Round Trip Home

ROUND TRIP HOME

Elizabeth Kouhi

Penumbra Press, 1983

Published by PENUMBRA PRESS, P.O. Box 340, Moonbeam,
Ontario, Canada POL IVO, with financial assistance from
The Canada Council and The Ontario Arts Council.

ISBN 0 920806 57 0

for my husband, George

BOREAL SUMMER

I hardly had time
To look carefully
At the violet
And the rose, and the
Warbler's yellow breast,
When already the aster
And the golden rod came
Crowding in and the
Warbler's feathers
Were bleached pale.

There it is, my childhood
Soft solstice, twilight —
Low-key pinks, mauves, yellows,
Smoldering
Through snow-clouds;
Colours washing tenderly
The snow-burdened
Winter trees. But where are all
The other watchers of those far off
Twilights? Where is the permanent world
Of my youth? Swept away, withered
Like the grass, or faded like
That image in my glass?

The calendar says the sun's
Turned toward us—but
There's no evidence of this
As I look into my garden:
The crab thrusts its stiff limbs
Outward; the raspberry canes
Lean dispiritedly and the lilacs
Stand rigid in the frosty air,
As if never to perfume the
World again. My kinsmen
On another northern shore
Have a special word for
These saturnine January days,
A word that bares the bleakness,
That weighs the soul with
Weary winter heaviness.

TO MY HUSBAND

It is not just a country
for the young, Mr Yeats;
this green August—
with odours of growth
scattering from the shores,
with water pressing our
flesh as the stars reign
after a blue-brilliant day—

this August
flows around and
in us and we pleasure in the
darkness of the sun-warmed lake,
free of early summer chills.

TO BRIAN ON WATCHING HIM ON TV

You were even then
Filled with energy, chaotic
And undirected; your mind
And body racked with
Restlessness.

You searched for ways to free
The genius clawing at you.
You wrote poetry but your
Long limbs hung from
Every corner.
For you, communication
Through eyes and brains
Of editors was tortuous;
and polishing treble clefs
Would have crippled you
Forever.

I watched you at work
Behind the footlights pushing
Young bodies, willing them into
Shapes and patterns of your creation;
I knew you had found
A lively art that left
No part of you unused.

ONE JULY MORNING

The misty
Grey morning
Is damply warm,
Unusual for our
Pre-Cambrian shield.

Burning coils chase
Mosquitoes; bird wings
Flutter.

I drink my
Wood-stove-brewed
Coffee and eat
Live-coal-toasted
Bread; green, and early
Summer fresh, the woods
Slope to the mist—
Hung lake; I read
Dorothy Livesay
(A book published
When she was sixty).

I peer through
Binoculars at a bird
And have my usual
Thurberish troubles. (I'm
Improving though)

She's accomplished
So much
In *her* sixty years.

But then (I tell myself)
At twenty five
She knew
There were
Modern poets
Other than
Masefield and
Edward Thomas.

A MANNIKIN IN THE MANITOBA MUSEUM

I must remind myself
You are just a hollow mannikin
Sitting there on an empty trunk,
Not your living counterpart—
A babushka-headed young woman
With carefully chosen possessions,
Facing a new life in a new world.

> *Where were you when they*
> *Crucified your Lord?*

I was young
(But not that young)
The city was redolent
With Maytime,
New — exciting.
The War? It was far away.
With others I sang
'The White Cliffs of Dover'
And 'When the Lights go
On again, All Over the World.'

> *Newspapers said enemy*
> *Aliens moved from coast*
> *Where were you when...?*

I was young
(But not that young)
The city redolent
With Maytime.
The War? We saw
Movies, black and white —
Heroes, villains.
It was comforting to
Be always right.

> *Newspapers said*
> *'Japs repatriated'*
> *Where were you?*
> *O where were you?*

Deaf and dumb
To cries in that
Maytime city.

TO THE YOUNG ARTISTS AT TOBERMORY (ONT.)

You work
To wrest
Order from chaos,
Forcing colours,
Fibres, clay
To shape your visions.

I regret that I gave
Nothing but words—
A poor return
For such remembered
Moments.

Like
   the back
      of a black beetle

The wet
    midnight
       city
        glistens.

Streaked
   carelessly
      by

Rubies
   emeralds
     and
       ambers.

DEFINITION

Sometimes I leave my
Warm, sunlit valley
And climb precipitous cliffs
To get a wider view
Of headlands, windswept waters,
Distant blue horizons.
Mostly I climb alone,
But there have been fleeting
Moments when response
From another
Has sharpened the eye
To awareness of shapes
And textures
And intensified the blueness
Of the far promontory.

ON READING
'A LONG APPRENTICESHIP'

—poems by Fred Cogswell

A few caused gongs
Inside my head; others
Tinkled little silvery bells;
But some reverberated through
Long corridors of memory
Causing me to nod my head and say,
'Yes, that's the way it was.'

T. M. AT A LIBRARY READING

A young poet stood at the podium
Ready for the reading; he took
A sip of water; he opened his
Mouth for the words to start
Flowing. Then he saw his audience—
Mostly sixtyish women, wrinkled,
Grey-haired, varicosed, looking
At him patiently, expectantly waiting.

A frantic scurry started behind his
Eyes. 'What'll I read to those old
Dears. I can't read them my naughty lines.'

'Oh, Sir Poet, rest your fears,
Rest your fears, under those wrinkles,
Inside those grey heads dwell
Variegated lives—purple,
And beige and red and yellow,
So just do your thing as you
Would at any other podium;
That's a good fellow.'

You as editor
Of the *Forge*
Gave me my
First rejection
Slip; you strove
To soften the action
By telling a mutual
Friend you liked
My smile.

As you sit there
Being questioned
I perceive we are
Still the same
Distance apart;
At McGill you lived
With Ezra Pound;
I was still with Keats.

Now you're read
In many languages,
You write 'close
To the bone'; I
Have a child's
Adventure book to
My name and still
Struggle in flesh
And fat.

But you *too*
Are growing old.

THE IMMIGRANT

Isanta, isanta come buy my fine pastries
Fine pastries for sale, fine pastries for sale!

    The market women's cries shrill sharply
    Through the hospital sounds—a man moans
    In the next bed, the floor polisher whines,
    The clattering of dishes and.............
    Antti lifts his feet lightly again on
    The cobbled market square in old Viipuri
    On the Baltic, the old seaport of Hansa
    Merchants, on the way to the Don.
    A young man in clumsy country linens excited
    By the hawkers' cries, by the stalls piled
    High with stuff—the mingled smell
    Of fish, spring lilac, new-made bread
    And the famous Viipuri pastries.

Isanta, isanta come buy my fine pastries
Fine pastries for sale, fine pastries for sale

    They call me isanta
    Master of my own land. Roots of centuries
    In the soil pulled out by the bailiff—
    The wagon loaded, the seven year old's
    Puzzlement, the gentle mother crying,
    The scattering of the large household;
    (Parents, brothers, sisters, aunts and divers help)
    I am not an isanta, I'm a renki ploughing
    Another man's fields. The nurse's cool
    Hand and a jab of a needle, the moaning
    In the next bed is louder.

They say there is free land in America;
A passport in three languages—Russian,
Swedish and Finnish, signed by
The provincial governor in the Grand
Duchy of Finland and stamped in Hango.

The man in the next bed is retching,
Hospital sounds clattering and clashing.
It was a stormy passage. The train dirty
And sooty from St John took endless days
Through the long forests. It stopped once in
The middle of the wilderness, for a half
Day it stood there.
Who has come to see me? My daughter?
My hands were blistered, then bloody from
Pushing the ore barrows and that
Is when I had the fever. Coppercliff.
Who are you? The rooming house woman?
You looked after me, a stranger
In a strange new land. They say I
Piled up all my bed clothes when at
The height of delirium. Rooming house
Woman don't kiss me and cry over me.

Everyone had a fever who came in those days.
That was no place for a man who wanted
Land—no green thing survived
Those deadly fumes. Men talked about
Homesteads around Port Arthur:
'Crown Lands Office, District of Thunder Bay
W.H. Hesson, agent, Port Arthur, Ontario
February nine nineteen hundred and five
Sir I have to inform you that you
Are located for the N½ lot 16 Concession 5
Gorham under the Free grant
And Homestead Act.' It was a sunny, clear day
When neighbour Jakki and I started
Out for the land that was ours.
Who is that man? My chest is burning
That man talks my language
'Miten Pappa voi?' How am I?
I am fine except for the burning.

It was a fine spring day, some snow still
Lay in the valleys, we carried
Bread, tea, butter and salt
An axe, a tea pail, a frying pan
And a change of socks.
A wagon trail made the first part
Easy going, past homesteads of my
Countrymen. Then we pressed northward
Watching for surveyors' posts, northward
Trails, mostly climbing over fallen trees left
From some forgotten forest fire.

Jakki found his land first and we spent our
First night camped at the elbow of
His river. We had a royal meal of
Rabbit and fresh spring trout.
This was better than any renki's life
We both agreed. No one told us what to do.
Is that you Liisa? You used to say I
Worked much harder than for any boss.
Why do you have on that white cap?
But then you were always inclined to
Fancy ways. Take that stone from my breast.
I can't breathe, why can't I move my hands?
Liisa don't speak to me in the other tongue....
It wasn't a bad life, was it?

We did build a farm, other
Countrymen came and it became part of
A place—a place to belong to. We had
Our own pihakoivut—birch trees in the yard.
Even when bad times came to all the land
Men without work rode the rods, from
Ocean to ocean. We were never hungry even
Though we saw no money. It wasn't a bad life
Was it Liisa? Why can't I move my
Hands? Why do you speak the other tongue?

You sent that boy into the city school
When I got too old and weak we had to sell....
No one to carry on, a few dollars left
From fifty years of work. The stone
Is pressing me again. My hands are
Heavy. There's that man again
He speaks my language, not the other tongue
I must go and cut some wood, it's cold
In here, the fire must be out.

Again the birch trees by the Vuoksi
Glitter in the sun. It's time to go
To the Viipuri market.

Isanta, isanta come buy my fine pastries
Fine pastries for sale, fine pastries for sale.

Mr Keats, how did you
Know it was
The Belle Dame
Sans Merci
Who left you
On that cold hillside?
And Mr Graves
In what way
Do you recognize
The White Goddess
Enslaving you?

I, too, have been visited
Here on my northern shore,
By phantoms awesome
Dread and marvelous,
But when I reach out
Nothing is left
And I am alone
With primordial mists
Slithering inside my skull.

LUCKY YEATS

Lucky Yeats, listening
To the lake water low-lapping
And the gentle pulse of linnet's wings—
No amplifying fools in his Innisfree.

Naked branches trace
Black patterns of death
On the grey slate
Of the Autumn sky.

> *Do you suppose the purple of my gloves*
> *Will match the purple of my hat?*

The muskeg is laid out
Cold and naked
On the heavy slab
Of rigid Autumn earth.

> *Where is Johnny taking you tonight?*
> *The movie at the Rialto is good, they say.*

The sap will run again
And the muskeg rise
From its sleep of death.

> *Do you think it will rain today?*
> *I'd hate to have my Easter bonnet spoiled.*

FRANCO AND THE LUMBERJACK

Two men lay dying
Each on his
Own continent

> Long-backed, stocky
> Hewers of wood
> Mattis, Jussis, Jaakkos

> Hewers of wood—yes!
> But not abject
> Hewers of wood.

> (Old minute books
> Record motions on
> Burning issues of the day)

> 'Workers of the World Arise
> Solidarity forever.'

One lay dying under white hospital
Sheets—wrinkled, weather-stained
Skin, gnarled fingers from
Frozen winters cutting pulp

> The old minute books speak
> Of plans
>   For May Day Parades
>   For strikes
>   For demonstrations
>   For raising money
>   for struggling Brothers
>   (Timmins, Minnesota Iron Range)

> Other paragraphs document
> Earnest discussions clarifying
> Objectives, stratagems against
> The Enemy.

Or small details of a Saturday night dance—
     Wax for the dance floor
     Price of tickets
     Appointing of clean-up crews.

In the El Pardo Palace built
In 1543 by Charles V the other
Lay dying, surrounded by teams
Of doctors, high officials, men of state—
Splendour, luxury.

          Then came the time to stand
          Behind all those motions
          And seconding of motions.

     To hold a gun.
               'Passport is valid for one year until
               April 6th 1938. In virtue of which this
               passport is given to entitle the bearer to
               proceed abroad without let or hindrance
               In token of which this official seal is
               herewith appended, this 6th day of
               April 1937.'

     Tourists on a passenger liner to Cherbourg
     Lumberjacks going to the Paris Exposition
     With people who ignore
     The approaching holocaust.

Most of the old comrades have gone.
A doctor looks in once a day
And nurses do what is needful
He fights his last fight.

Nightmarish
Clambering
Over the Pyrennees
To the Republic Espanola.
Arrival finally
To the cheering and oranges
From the loyal people and
From comrades in
The Brigades Internationales.
(MacKenzie-Papineau Bat.)

Issued with a
Carnet Militar Para
A strange life began an

Out-of-focus dream with
Startling clarities

   The pressure of rope sandals
   (on feet used to lumberjack boots)
   The smell of gunfire
   On the Ebro; the
   Frightening chaos of retreats;
   The bone-weariness of forced marches;
   The aching heave of the pick
   On fortifications—remembered

   Together with the caress
   Of the warm pavement under foot,
   (And other softer caresses)
   The gay non-soldier crowds;
   And the first dinner
   On a Barcelona leave.

Daily communiques are issued
From the sixteenth century
Castle, the world awaits
For news of the last old man

Two years (Did immigration ignore the
original date on the passport?) of

Fighting
Fleeing
Digging
Marching—

Thus moving and seconding
With two years of life
Those minute book resolutions.

From the Republic, many gracias and
A welcome from a few comrades as he
Arrived home. But no official accolades
no honours
no ribbons

As for men returning from the same war
A few years later; dead comrades did not
Get their names carved into
Remembrance stones to be bugled
Once a year.

The fight is over and the
Nurse pulls the final curtain
Around his bed in the public ward
The last communique comes from
El Pardo Palace.

The big communal tables have gone
And the clientele is largely
White collar or expensive blue
Experiencing ethnic eating.

An aged pulpcutter shambles
in: he
remembers eating
his fill
for a quarter at
the big tables—
              Old Home Fare
              Meat in gravy
              Potatoes
              Suolakala
              Viili
              Turnip Loaf
              Carrots and Beets
              and home-made
              Bread, Sweet Soup
              and Pies for dessert

when the place
was a
Co-op and the
building
The Labour Temple.
Or maybe, he remembers
coming in for coffee
after a fierce political
meeting
(Still simmering over the
Fascists in Spain)
or after a May Day parade
or from being chased by
the Police on a picket line.

Do the white and the expensive blue sitting
At their tables, eating ethnic foods
Notice the old man who helped win
For them the life-style they now enjoy?

THE ARTIST

Is that what you really saw—
Cool, candy-coloured rocks
Sitting prettily in the landscape?
Are those the blizzard-battered,
Frost scarred outcroppings
From the harsh Pre-Cambrian earth,
Named in the titles of your canvases?

No—you knew that Toronto living
Rooms could not withstand the northern truth.

ON READING P.K. PAGE BEFORE A CONCERT

I touch and turn and rub
With my fingertips, my palms,
Feel the polished surfaces,
The honed edges; I see
The emeralds, sapphires
And the tourmaline begin to glow;
Prisms reflecting and re-reflecting
Lights and colours, just as
The flutes, the clarinets and
French horns begin to throw
Crystal notes at me, suggesting
Worlds within worlds, within worlds.

THE WEDDING

The lights dim. The first bar
of music announces the waltz
for the couple. Replete after
the festal board of pasta
ribs salads cabbage rolls roast
beef pickled herring fried chicken
salt cured salmon and fancy desserts,
the wedding guests (clusters of
faces, not Brueghel uniform, dark
Mediterranean and Baltic pale
and others in between) watch
the pair in foreplay
for the mingling of bloods
the making of a nation.

'You never knew who would come
To the door at night, out of the darkness,
From the howling wilderness to look
For shelter and we'd heard stories
Of terrible things, of blood and fire.
Yet, there stood the injunction in
Burning letters *Be Ye Hospitable*.
So I devised a room, small,
Windowless, with an opening to our
Strong son's room. It was
Dry, and warm as the rest of the house
With a bed and covers, better than
The ground outside in the frost or rain.'

Kitchener, 1982

The Pleiads sparkled
Around my head; the train
Of Aldebaran caught
Me in its tow; I danced
On the Milky Way, I tip-
Toed inside a crimson
Petal and dove into a
Crystal raindrop—Adam and
Jonathan, Peter and Augustine
Welcomed me; my great, great
Great grandchildren embraced
Me as I leaned forward on the
Rail to eat, and held the
Goblet to my lips to drink.

IN THE SCUOLA A GRANDE DI SAN ROCCO

for Francesco

In the Scuola a Grande di San Rocco
The tourists stand before Tintoretto.

> *A figure suffused in*
> *Puissant light stands*
> *Accusing his accusers*
> *By his gentle curves*
> *And soft lines;*
> *Pilate is washing his hands.*

The sophisticate, the lover of Art,
The temperamental Latin (who
does not suffer fools gladly, or
even some not fools)
Describes Tintoretto's techniques,
Pauses, suddenly becomes a
Passionate advocate for the
Tortured ones of the world.
He stands transformed.

> *Were men redeemed to*
> *Pull out each other's toe nails?*
> *Shall we keep washing*
> *Our hands?*

RETURNING

My head like a daliesque filing drawer,
overstuffed by images, garnered
along the way, aches for the
understanding of its burden:

The Titian reds,
violets, blues
embraceable in
magic light;
Spirits ascending
with Gothic arches;
Far worlds beckoning
behind Madonnas;
Disquieting St John
the Baptist, beard
split, hair wild;
In the Botticelli
'Spring' lines and
colours delicately
addressing the soul;
Exquisitely soothing
symmetry of the Renaissance
lines and circles;
Michelangelo as Joseph
in the Duomo Pieta
brooding in
soul-breaking darkness.

But I keep returning around the corner
to end my journey with Della Robbia's
lovely singing children and Donatello's
dancing angels.
'Laudate Dominum in Sanctis eius.'

CHAGALL IN ZURICH

I longed to hear your
Words that afternoon,
When the sun shone
Through the magic
Windows of Chagall.
I wanted you to tell
Me what you saw and
Felt. But I dared not
Ask because our years
Got in the way.

If only there had been
A crowd of other tourists,
I could have hidden from
The dispassionate young
Curator. He went on
(pretending not to notice)
To explain the reasons
For the narrow, corridor-like room:
'In those days, Roman law decreed
That a room had to be stripped,
The furniture burned after a
Consumptive death and Severn,
His friend who was nursing him.......

(*We who in these antiseptic days greet*
Death in a sterile hospital rooms,
Can hardly imagine a friend performing
Tasks done today by paid labour.)

.....he had to bear the cost.
Only the ceiling beams and carved
Fireplace are the same as then.'

Did the twenty-six
Year old poet
(My own daughter's age),
I wondered, count
Those dark beams
As he lay dying
During that bleak
Roman winter?

(No beakers of the warm south here)
Or perhaps trace
With fragile fingers
The rigid flora
Of the mantlepiece?
(Amongst which no nightingale could sing)
The young man continued:
(Carefully averting his eyes)
'Sometimes on the sly Severn carried
Him into the larger room to hear the piano.
And Severn read Fanny's letters and marked
Them plus or minus to indicate her state.
The poet could no longer endure directly
The beloved contact.'

No surreptitious wiping hand
Could flick away the
Swelling wetness
From my nose and eyes.
(A foolish, middle-aged woman tourist)

Rome, 1976

Another Giovanni?
                (Father of Cosimo?)
But did
you
commission
                modern Brunelleschis

to create
immortal
works of art?

                (or even mortal works?)

Perhaps
you
deserve
those grim grey basins.

They are like women from the subterranean
Caverns of my mind — women with strong
Rough hands, hair pulled back in sensible
Buns, faces innocent of creams and lotions,
Women who walked a straight row, talked
Eye to eye with their men — Pre-Cambrian
Sisters to the Yorkshire women
Resurrected here.

You sheathe yourself with much
Fraternal paraphernalia;
Snowmobiles, cars, bridge games
And hunting guns—like some
Kind of bulky space suit,
To protect your poet's heart
That was brought into this
World by an M.D. in return for
Three Mountain Ash Trees.

As the Romans strain
At the puppet strings,
My head draws
Back and I gaze
Upward at them.

Cimabue and Ducio
Dangle me somewhere
Chagall-like in mid-air
But Giotto lets my feet rest
Firmly on the floor, and
My eyes stare straight ahead.

ROUND TRIP HOME

It holds back the line
Of birch, spruce and pine—
The long, lonely highway
Bordered by daisies, asters,
Pink and yellow clover.
In the distance, royal blue
Superior shimmers, purple
Headlands brood and green
Nearer shores quiver in
The sunlight, as we ride by.

II

We rest in the gently coloured pale lime
And yellow evening, sipping our after
Dinner tea, allowing the quiet time
Still the pounding wheels from our nerve's centre.
The warm breeze, the running Aux Sables water,
The clear fluting bird song in the pine
All help to heal the bruised tension line.

For half a century logs tumbled down
The Aux Sables. Lumberjacks ate
Pork and beans and slept in hoar-
Frosted cabins and perched on
Cross-beams. In Old Ontario
Imitation English manors were built.

We soon forget
The cold behinds
As we curl
Warmly inside our
Sleeping bags,
Within our blue
And orange
Tent, with
Teen agers and
Motorcyclists as
Our neighbours.
Other Seniors
Are elsewhere
In the Park.

Later in the night I try
To explain to the ghostly
Lumberjack who's come to
Haunt me that today he'd
Have indoor plumbing, carpets
And a table packed with food.

III

Coppercliff slag heaps, mountains of
The moon—Father's 1902 bloody,
Blistered ore-barrow hands.

IV

My childhood curiosity
Quickens on Highway Sixty Nine:
'Where does that road go?'
I would ask my father.
When will we have the time
To follow the beckoning
Of all those road signs—
Byng, Bayfield, Point au Baril,
Moon River, Beausoleil and Honey Harbour—
All the road signs of the world?

V

An evening stroll along the boardwalk
On Lake Ont.—hum of the city in the
Distance but the water, trees and grass
Keep the Concrete Monster in abeyance.

VI

Sunday afternoon at Kleinburg
With green pines, greenness all around.

Inside:
>   The miraculous whimsy
>   Of Inuit sculptures—
>   Whimsy born in sixty
>   Below temperatures.
>   I walk lightly.
>   I would skip and hop
>   If I weren't sixty,
>   As I leave the two laughing
>   Walruses battling.
>
>   A.Y. Jackson's familiar contours
>   Of the north.
>
>   Gentle, subtle, soft violets
>   Greys and light greens of Fitzgerald.
>
>   Semi-oriental white, blue-grey
>   Worlds of David Milne.
>
>   No laughing walruses battle in
>   Harris's Arctic landscapes.
>
>   Emily Carr's green life seething
>   Sends ripples of near-fear up my spine.
>
>   Dear Tom T.—You've gathered my
>   Country into your canvases.

VII

We take a river boat
Up the Niagara to Lewiston
And back. We float
Where LaSalle and Hennepin
Journeyed to explore
The new world, but we're
Tourists and it's nineteen
Seventy nine, we've seen
These shores before
And there's Love Canal.

VIII

Soft summer evening, the rising orange
Moon glancing subtle light over the
Tops of the tall corn, horses moving
In the orchard, the unbearable
Sweetness of new-mown hay.

IX

As we glide up the river we see the banks
Crayoned in green, purple, yellow and gold,
Wooded, flowered as they were before, thanks
To Joseph's people who have not sold
Their inheritance to bull dozers
Builders of smoke stacks and other spoilers.

'Way down up de Swanee River
Far, far away, dere's where
My heart is turning ever.'

What's wrong with the Grand?

Let me tell you a story
A story from our land
A story of a river
That is called the Grand.

It was the year of the War
Of Eighteen Twelve when two
Yankee soldiers travelled far
Up the Grand, as they flew
Away from their duty
With a payroll as their booty
And hid it in the forests by the Grand.

They flew from duty
With their booty
And hid it, hid it
By the Grand.

> Not about the Blue Ohio or the
> Wabash awash.

About the brave Chief Brant
Who got beaten because he
Stood up to the Yank;
Or about the poet Pauline
Who made herself a name
And the runner Tom
Longboat who gathered fame,
All from the banks of the Grand,
The Grand, the Grand, all from
The banks of the Grand.

(Will the real singers please take over!)

X

We followed the well-worn tourist
Track to see Jack Falstaff poke
Fun at honour, and Othello
Smother Desdemona.

XI

Through horse and buggy country
To Fergus and Elora and strong
Stone houses built by early Scots
Masons—houses sturdy, four-square,
Built to stand several generations.
We ate Canadian food—pita bread
With curried filling and found
Something for our myth-makers
In a little Elora church—Florence
Nightingale's gift of communion
Ware to her cleric lover.
(How our neighbours would have sung!)

XII

A historic plaque signals to us on the
Highway. On a little knoll we find
A Women's Institute memorial for a
Local daughter. Near here, it announces
Was born Nellie Mooney McClung in 1873
And left with her family for the West in 1880.

XIII

We came this way
To chase a memory,
A memory of a little
Black and white
Picture in a
Childhood geography text—
Flower Pots in Georgian
Bay.

As the tourist launch
Circles the island,
We see that memory
Does not exactly
Match reality.

XIV

Manitoulin
Dwelling place
Of Gitchi Manitou
The sacred Isle—
Sold for thirty
Pieces of silver.

XV

We finally reach a high point, after hours
Of climbing the rocky Pre-Cambrian shield
And there in the distance of flashes Superior
Great Superior, superior of lakes, that can wield
A wicked wave that snaps ships in half
And in black rage pommels its coastal cliffs
Into strange shapes, but can also laugh,
Glimmer and shimmer and gently lift
Its waters to caress the long sandy shores
Or enchant us with the glorious pageantry
Of everchanging kaleidoscope of emeralds, azures.
I want to celebrate your invincibility!
Then I remember the flowing streams of sludge
That have already assailed your edge.

LOOKING FOR THE MOON
A Rhyming Poem for Children

Nora and Daddy strolled
Down the street, down the street,
On their way to try to meet,
To try to meet
Old Mr Moon.

They looked up,
And they looked around
Above the tree tops
And chimney pots
But Mr Moon could not be found,
Could not be found.

Nora cried 'til tears flowed down
'Where is Mr Moon? Mr Moon's not around.'
Daddy exclaimed: 'The rascal, he's hiding himself!
We'll have to come on another night,
On another night.'

On another night they went out,
Strolling down the street,
Down the street.
They looked around
Above the tree tops,
And the chimney pots.
'Look' said Daddy, 'look up there.'
His fingers pointed way up high,
Where a crescent moon hung up in the sky.
Nora laughed and laughed.
'Mr Moon's come out of hiding,' she said.
'Hello Mr Moon, hello. I'm so glad to see you way up there.'

Nora and Daddy stood on the street
And looked at the moon way up high,
Above the tree tops
And chimney pots.
'But why are you so thin Mr Moon?' Nora cried.
'Do you not get enough to eat?'
Mr Moon said nothing, but Daddy explained,
'He's there all right, big, round and fat,
But he's still playing a game with you,
He's playing peak-a-boo.'
Nora laughed and said, 'ooh, ooh,
I want to see him round and fat.'
Daddy said: 'We'll come another night,
We'll come another night.'

On another night they went out
Strolling down the street,
Down the street.
They looked around
Above the tree tops
And the chimney pots.
'Look,' said Daddy, 'look up there.'
And there was the moon
Hanging way up in the sky.
Nora clapped her hands in glee.
'It is, it is fat and round,' said she.
But Daddy said: 'Look at it, look carefully,
And you will see that Mr Moon is hiding
A tiny piece of himself. He's like a
Puzzle that's still not done.'

Nora frowned and said, 'Oh,
He's still not fat and round.
Why isn't he?' And she stood straight
Up with her arms akimbo and said.
'Mr Moon, I've waited and waited for you
To grow big and fat and round.
Please Mr Moon, isn't it time?'

Mr Moon said nothing,
But Daddy explained. 'He's got his own
Rhythm, he's got his own pace.
We just have to wait to see his full face.'
But Nora was angry and stomped off to bed.
'I'm tired of waiting for him to grow fat.
He's a silly old Moon.' She said.

A few nights later,
Nora forgot her anger,
And she and Daddy again went
Strolling down the street,
Down the street.
And they looked around
Above the tree tops
And the chimney pots.
'Look' said Daddy, 'look up there.'
His fingers pointed way up high
Where a fat, round moon
Hung up in the sky.
Nora laughed and laughed.
'Mr Moon's full grown, hello Mr Moon.
I'm glad you're big and fat and round.'

RECENT TITLES IN THE PENUMBRA PRESS POETRY SERIES

ANN FOX CHANDONNET *Auras Tendrils (Poems of the North)*
   ISBN 0 920806 45 7

DEBORAH GODIN *Stranded in Terra*
   ISBN 0 920806 53 8

MARY WEYMARK GOSS *In Hiding*
   ISBN 0 920806 54 6

NEILE GRAHAM *Seven Robins*
   ISBN 0 920806 55 4

M.T. KELLY *Country You Can't Walk In and Other Poems*
   ISBN 0 920806 56 2

ELIZABETH KOUHI *Round Trip Home*
   ISBN 0 920806 57 0

J. MICHAEL YATES *Insel: The Queen Charlotte Islands Meditations*
   ISBN 0 920806 58 9